Whiskers and Paws

Poems chosen by Fiona Waters

Illustrated by Vanessa Julian-O

MATHEW PRICE LIMITED

I Met a Cat

I met a cat and he was magic
So he played a fiddle for me
And I danced with him to the music
Until it was half past 3.

Daniel Payne

Only my Opinion

Is a caterpillar ticklish?
Well, it's always my belief
That he giggles, as he wiggles
Across a hairy leaf.

Monica Shannon

Polar Bear

The secret of the polar bear
Is that he wears long underwear.

Gail Kredenser

Higglety, Pigglety, Pop!

Higglety, pigglety, pop!
The dog has eaten the mop;
The pig's in a hurry,
The cat's in a flurry,
Higglety, pigglety, pop!

Anon

You Can't Catch Me!

I'm a velvety mole
My home is a hole
I'm not very big
But I do like to dig
I'll spoil your lawn
But I'm gone by dawn
I chuckle with glee
For you can't catch me!

Clare Rhodes

The Mouse

There's such a tiny little mouse
Living safely in my house.
  Out at night he'll softly creep,
  When everyone is fast asleep.
    But always in the light of day
    He softly, softly creeps away.

Thirza Wakley

Rat a Tat Tat

Rat a tat tat, who is that?
Only grandma's pussy cat.
What do you want?
A pint of milk.
Where's your money?
In my pocket.
Where's your pocket?
I forgot it.
O you silly pussy cat!

Anon

Hickety Pickety

Hickety Pickety
My black hen
She lays eggs
For gentlemen.
Sometimes nine
And sometimes ten.
Hickety Pickety
My black hen.

Anon

Tiger

I'm a tiger
Striped with fur
    Don't come near
      Or I might Grrr
        Don't come near
          Or I might growl
            Don't come near
              Or I might BITE!

Mary Ann Hoberman

He and She

He was a rat, and she was a rat,
And down in one hole did they dwell,
And both were as black as a witch's cat,
And they loved one another well.

Anon

White Sheep

White sheep, white sheep
On a blue hill,
When the wind stops
You all stand still.
You all run away
When the winds blow;
White sheep, white sheep,
Where do you go?

Anon

For Guinness, the best of cats
F M W
For Barbara and Derek
V J - O

For permission to reproduce copyright material, acknowledgement and thanks are due to the following:
Daniel Payne for 'I Met a Cat"; Monica Shannon and Doubleday & Co. Inc. for 'Only my Opinion'
from *Goose Grass Rhymes*; Clare Rhodes for 'You can't catch me!'; Thirza Wakley and Unwin Hyman for 'The Mouse' from
The Book of a Thousand Poems; Mary Ann Hobermann and Russell and Volkening Inc. for 'Tiger'
from *Hello and Goodbye* published by Little Brown Inc.
Every effort has been made to trace copyright but if any omissions have been made please
let us know in order that we may put them right in the next edition.

This compilation copyright © Fiona Waters 1990, 2003
Illustrations copyright © Vanessa Julian-Ottie 1990
First published 1990 by Hodder and Stoughton Children's Books
This edition published 2003 by Mathew Price Limited
The Old Glove Factory, Bristol Road, Sherborne, Dorset DT9 4HP
ISBN 1-84248-064-2 (hardback)
ISBN 1-84248-063-4 (paperback)
Printed in China

WHAT MAISIE DID NEXT

Author and illustrator: Aileen Paterson

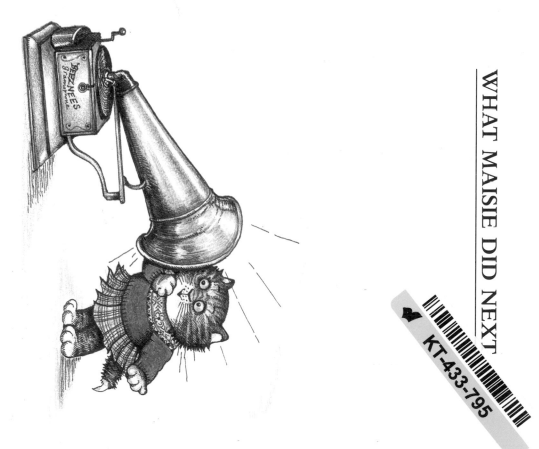

This story is dedicated to friends, Willie and Victoria Reid, Peggy Shiels and Kay Johnston, with my apologies for always being so busy!

Thanks to my son, Liam Paterson, for help with research at the Museum.

The publishers wish to acknowledge the help and co-operation of Directors and staff of The Royal Scottish Museum, Chambers Street, Edinburgh.

© Aileen Paterson

Published in 1991 by
The Amaising Publishing House Ltd.
Musselburgh
EH21 7UJ
Scotland

031-665 8237

Reprinted 1993
Printed & Bound by Scotprint Ltd, Musselburgh

ISBN 1 871512 09 3

Other Maisie Titles in the Series:

Maisie goes to School

Maisie and the Posties

Maisie's Festival Adventure

Maisie loves Paris

Maisie and the Space Invader

Maisie in the Rainforest

Maisie goes to Hospital

Maisie and the Puffer

Winter can be a dreary time of year once Christmas is over. Some animals are lucky and sleep right through it, but not cats and kittens.

Maisie MacKenzie is a little tabby kitten who lives in Edinburgh, and one February she wished that Granny would let her stay in bed till the Easter holidays arrived.

She was fed up with Winter.

She was fed up with the wind and the rain, and wearing woolly vests, and not being allowed out to play after school. Her Daddy, a famous explorer, had come home for Christmas, but he was off on his travels again, to sunny Africa!

Maisie grew very bored and lazy. Her room got very untidy.

One Saturday afternoon, Granny put her foot down, with a firm paw.

"What a guddle in here!" she cried. She fetched the vacuum cleaner, furniture polish, and a feather duster. "Now Maisie," she said, "I'm away to do my baking. When I come back, I expect to find this place TICKETYBOO!"

"What a funny name for a place, Granny."

"No Maisie, I mean your room is to be clean and tidy," replied Granny!

Half an hour later, Granny's doorbell rang. Maisie didn't hear it. She was lying underneath her bed reading a comic she'd found there. The tidy-up had not got very far. But she did hear when Granny knocked on her door. "Nearly finished, Maisie? Mrs McKitty is here. She would like to take you to the Museum."

Mrs McKitty is Granny's neighbour, and a very pernickety pussycat.

"Er, nearly finished, Granny," gasped Maisie, wriggling out from under the bed.

"MRS McKITTY!!!" meowed Maisie. "I do hope she won't come in here. She can spot a speck of dust a hundred yards away!" She ran about in a panic, throwing toys in her toybox, and everything else into the cupboard.

Suddenly there was another knock at the door. It opened slowly.

Maisie's heart stood still . . . .

"Hello Maisie," said a voice.

Maisie sighed with relief. It was Archie, her best friend.

"What are you doing here?" she asked. "Are you going to the Museum with Mrs McKitty?" Archie nodded.

"Mrs McKitty made me an offer I couldn't refuse. My football landed in her window box. If I don't go she might confiscate it. Please come too." Maisie said she would. She took his paw and they came out to join Granny and Mrs McKitty.

Granny waved goodbye to them from the window as they went off to catch the 23 bus. She took her scones out of the oven, and was just going to sit down to read her library book, when she remembered Maisie's room. "I'll just see what a good job Maisie made of tidying up," she said to herself.

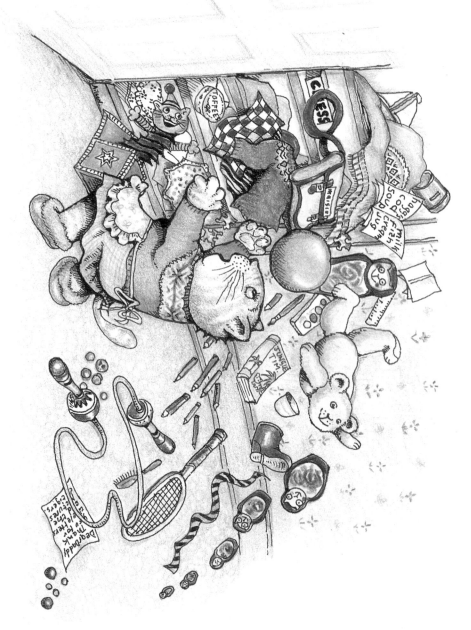

She was in for a shock! The carpet was all dusty, the bed was all lumpy. Under the bed she found the comic, two pence, bits of jigsaw, a wellyboot, and lots of fluff! And when she opened the cupboard door, everything shot out and landed on top of her. Maisie's teddy bear flew past as if he had wings!

Poor Granny spent the afternoon cleaning up, instead of sitting by the fire, having a rest.

There was not much rest for the kittens either, when they reached the Museum. Mrs McKitty brushed their fur, and inspected their paws and whiskers, then marched them up the steps. Maisie was quiet as she gazed around her in the huge main hall. Outside it was Winter, but in here it was like Spring. The Museum was like a glass palace.

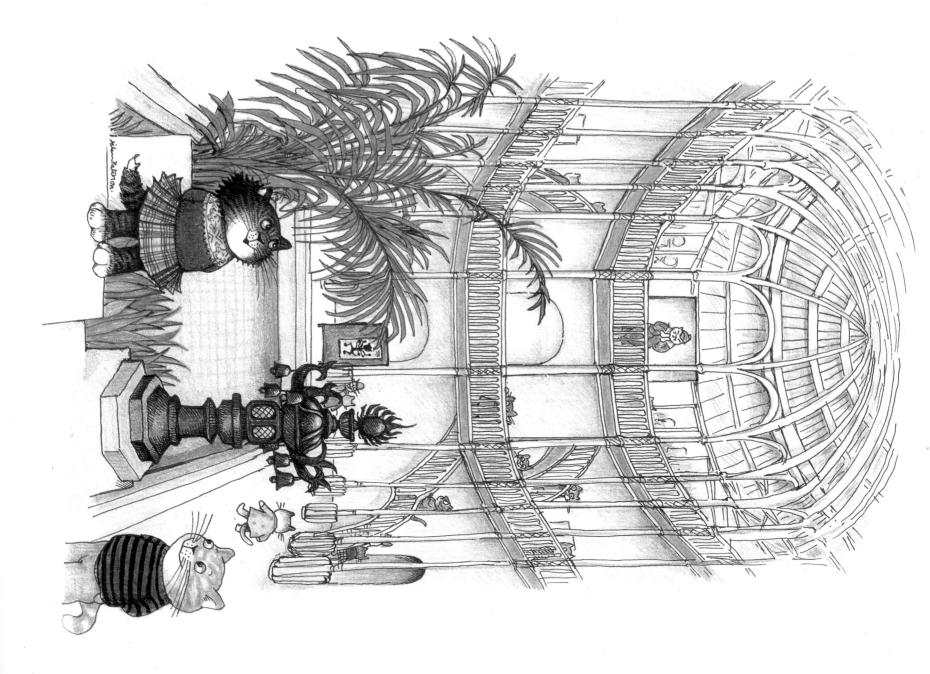

Her silence did not last for long. She and Archie soon began to bubble over with excitement.

"Look, a shop! Can we buy things?"

"There's a pond! Can we paddle?"

"Look over there, Mrs McKitty, there's a tea room! Let's have some ice-cream!"

"May we please go to see the engines, Mrs McKitty?" asked Archie.

"You press the buttons and the wheels go round. It's great fun!"

Mrs McKitty banged her umbrella on the floor. Her face was like a thunder cloud.

"FUN! You are not here to have fun, Archibald! Take Maisie's paw and follow me, and not another word from either of you. You are here to LISTEN and LEARN!"

She set off at a brisk pace carrying a list in her paw. Maisie and Archie scurried behind her, trying to keep up. They were rushed past lots of interesting things because they were not on the list. In and out, upstairs and downstairs, they followed, while Mrs McKitty did all the talking.

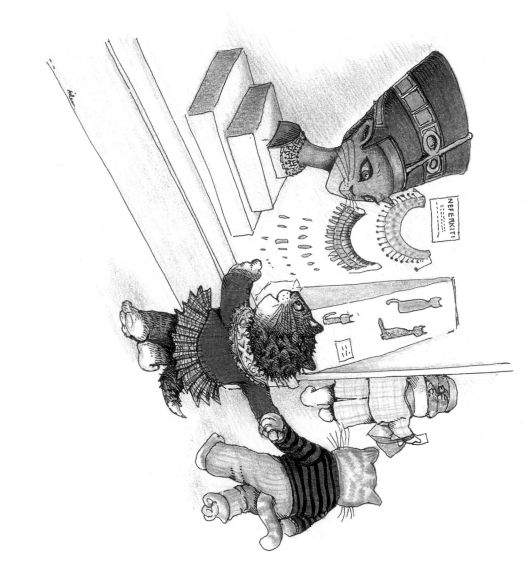

They looked at silver dishes in a case. Mrs McKitty said they were nearly as nice as her silver teapot. It was an heirloom, and had once belonged to her Auntie Nettie who had been forty years in the Post Office. (It must have been a very long queue, thought Maisie.)

On the top floor they saw the Chinese vases, but Mrs McKitty said that they were not a patch on the contents of her china cabinet. Her collection of Catto-di-Monty ornaments was the best in Edinburgh.

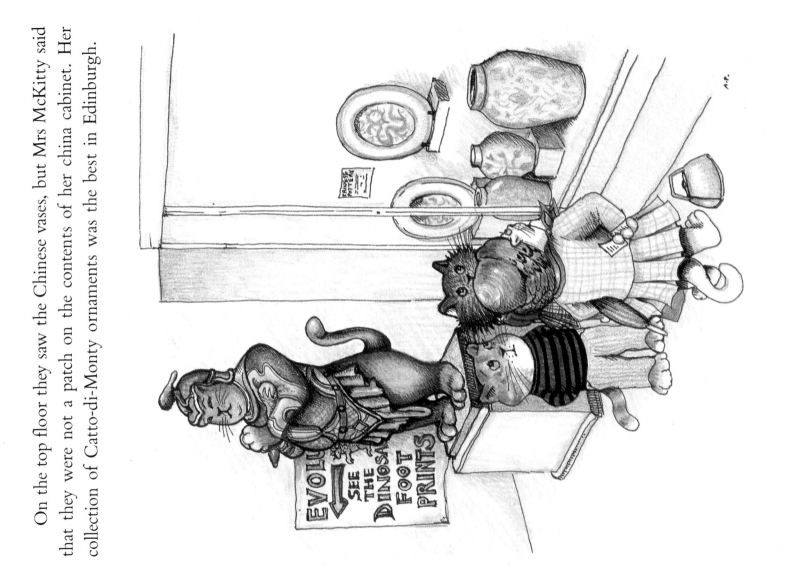

They gazed in horror at a roomful of bugs and beetles. Mrs McKitty said that if it was not for her scrubbing the stairs every day, they would all be up to their eyes in such ghastly beasties! None of her neighbours seemed to bother their ginger, she said.

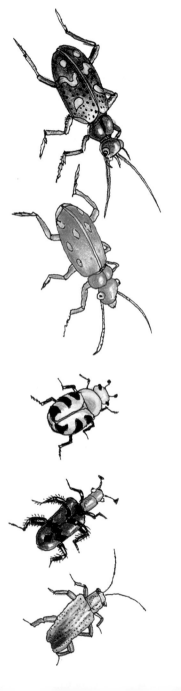

Archie and Maisie sighed. They were not enjoying this tour very much.

Archie wished he could play with the engines, and Maisie was tired of keeping quiet for so long. They were both thinking that Mrs McKitty had no idea how to enjoy the Museum, but they were in for a surprise . . .!

There was a special exhibition downstairs called 'The Good Old Days'.

There was plenty to see.

Funny bicycles called 'Pennyfarthings'.

Bathing suits as big, warm, and cosy as winter coats.

Photographs of trams and steam trains, and much, much more.

The kittens brightened up. It was all very interesting. Even Mrs McKitty stopped talking, and sighed, remembering long ago.

13

Exhibition Hall

The Good Old Days. 1800–1950

One display was called 'The Roaring Twenties'. Maisie smiled when she saw the strange clothes. She wondered if Granny had ever worn a frock covered with fringes, or a scarf made of feathers . . . or a hat like an upside-down flower pot! There was a gramophone on show. While she was looking inside the big horn, the museum attendant wound up the handle. She jumped back in surprise when loud music came out of the horn! But Mrs McKitty laughed with delight, and began to tap her paws in time to the catchy tune.

"My, my, my," she cried. "This takes me back to when I was the star of the Silver Slipper Ballroom. I was a *lovely* dancer . . . Mr McKitty used to call me 'Twinkletoes'. Just watch this!"

14

The kittens couldn't believe their eyes. Mrs McKitty burst into song and began dancing round the room, twirling her umbrella.

"I'm singing in the rain, just singing in the rain,
What a glorious feeling, I'm hap-hap-happy again . . ."

At last the two wee kittens could speak to one another.

"Well I Never!" they said, and burst out laughing.

A crowd of cats gathered round, clapping and cheering. The attendant joined in the fun by asking Mrs McKitty to dance 'The Foxtrot' with him! Maisie and Archie slipped outside into the main hall. They felt like having some fun of their own.

"How about a quick game of Hide-and-seek till Mrs McKitty comes out?" asked Archie.

"Good idea!" said Maisie. "I will hide somewhere on the ground floor while you count up to one hundred."

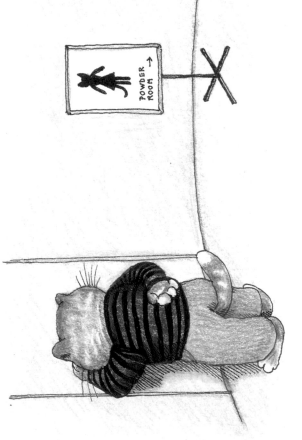

She found a good hidey-hole near the tea room. There were painters in that week to redecorate the museum, and they had left pots of paint, a ladder, and some dust sheets, in a corner. Maisie thought she would hide under the sheets. It should not take Archie too long to come and find her there. There was a radiator nearby, so it was cosy. She curled up and waited.

Archie finished counting and set out to find Maisie. He looked in all the galleries, in the shop, and behind the palms by the pond. He was just going to investigate the tea room, when a bell rang. It was time for the Museum to close. Lots of cats and kittens began heading for the big doors.

There was Mrs McKitty!

She was very angry when Archie told her that Maisie was hiding. They searched everywhere and called Maisie's name, but she was not to be seen. They told the attendants and described what Maisie was wearing, and they looked for her too. Then the doorkeeper dashed up to tell Mrs McKitty that he had seen a kitten in a purple jersey and kilt amongst the crowd. The kitten had left just a moment ago. Was it possible that Maisie had gone home on her own?

"With Maisie MacKenzie, anything is possible!" cried Mrs McKitty. "She must have missed us. Come, Archie, we may catch her at the Bus Stop. My poor nerves are on their last legs with all this worry."

Mrs McKitty and Archie left. The museum staff left. The lights were out. The doors were locked. All was quiet.

Now, it is true that a kitten in a purple jersey and kilt had left the Museum, but it was NOT Maisie! It was a kitten called Angus MacNab, and he did look rather like Maisie. He even lived in Morningside!

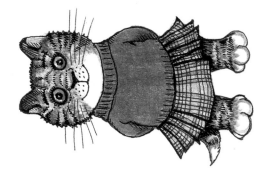

MAISIE WAS STILL IN THE MUSEUM, FAST ASLEEP!

She awoke with a start and remembered the game. She must have dozed off. Now she would have to go and find Archie!

What a shock she got when she poked her head out of the sheets. It was so dark that she could not see anything at first! She was very frightened. She meowed loudly, but no one answered.

Maisie realised that everyone must have gone home . . . .

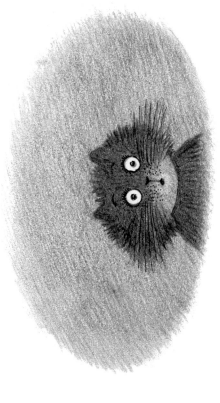

She lay still for a while, wondering what to do. Then she thought about her Daddy. What would he do? He was never afraid, because he was a fearless explorer. If she wanted to be an explorer too, she would have to find her way out of this fix. There was enough light shining through the glass roof for her to see a doorway. She crawled out and began to make her way towards it, holding on to the wall. She followed the wall till it turned a corner. Maisie looked round the corner, and gave a loud SCREECH!!

A big yellow tiger was leaping towards her!

She put out her paws in alarm . . . and touched a glass case.

"Silly sausage," she laughed. "He's nothing but a stuffed old tiger from the Museum."

There were lots more stuffed animals around her. She could see elephants and crocodiles standing in the gloom. There was even a little dragon! Maisie felt just like an explorer now, alone in the jungle at night.

She noticed a huge horned animal she had never seen before. The notice said he was an Alaskan moose. Maisie was amazed! The Scottish 'moose' is a tiny wee creature, who likes cheese.

She got another surprise. The skeleton of a vast Blue whale hung from the ceiling above her. Maisie had never seen anything like it.

"Goodness me," she said to herself. "What a big fish! I wonder if it could be an Alaskan haddock?"

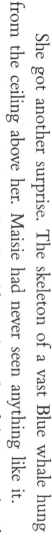

At last she made her way into the main hall. There on the wall above her were light switches. Maisie jumped up and down till she had managed to put them all on. Light filled the Museum. Now she could see everything properly.

As she passed the pond, she noticed that there were fish swimming around. She jumped in to have a closer look. The fish rushed off and hid behind the plants. Maisie splashed about trying to find them, but they were very good at Hide-and-seek. She made a lot of puddles with her splashing, and when she jumped out again, she left a trail of wet pawprints everywhere.

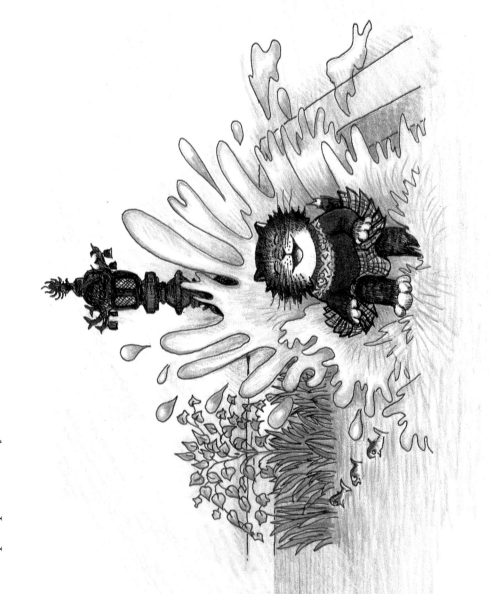

Paddling is good fun, she thought, but now she must think of how to get home.

Granny must be very worried.

She was walking past the Museum shop when she had a bright idea. She went inside and looked around. YES! There was a telephone on the counter!

Maisie dialled 999, and asked for the Police.

Sergeant MacStooshie answered.

Maisie told him her name and said she was stuck in the Museum and needed rescuing.

"We will be there in two ticks, Maisie," he said, "and we will bring your Granny."

"Do you know my Granny?" asked Maisie.

Sergeant MacStooshie laughed. "Your Granny has just phoned to say Mrs McKitty came home without you. I will tell her you are fine." Maisie sat down to wait . . . but after two ticks of the clock, she went off to do more exploring till Granny and the Police came.

Meanwhile Sergeant MacStooshie drove to Morningside and collected Granny. Mrs McKitty and Archie came too. When they arrived outside the Museum, Doctor Purrkins the Director of the Museum, was waiting for them with the keys to the big doors.

They rushed up the steps and looked around. There was no sight of Maisie, but there were signs that she was not far away! They could hear her singing!

The Gramophone was playing . . . "Happy Days Are Here Again!" and all over the floor were muddy pawprints and tracks.

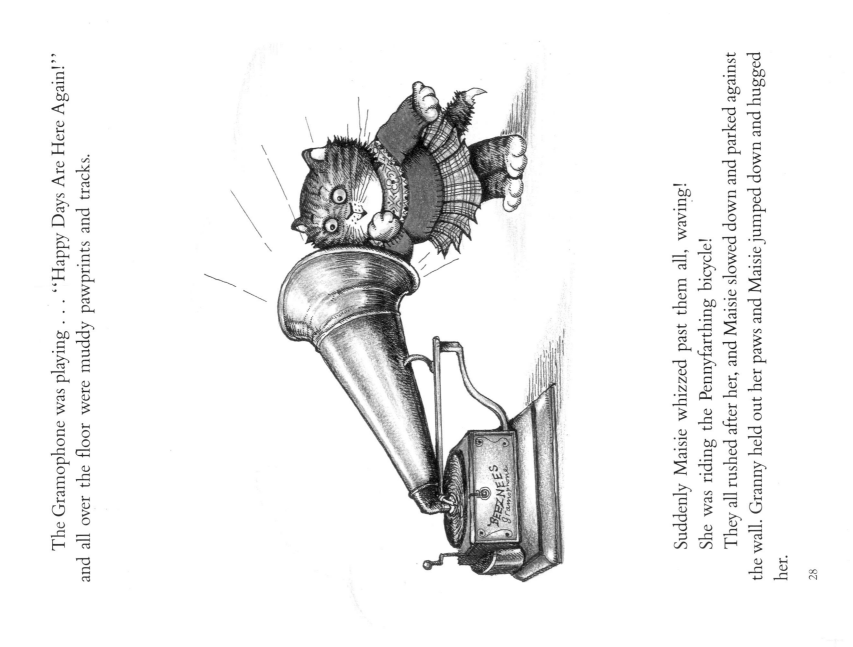

Suddenly Maisie whizzed past them all, waving!
She was riding the Pennyfarthing bicycle!
They all rushed after her, and Maisie slowed down and parked against the wall. Granny held out her paws and Maisie jumped down and hugged her.

"Hello Granny," she said. "Hello Archie. Hello Mrs McKitty."

Archie smiled. He was so pleased to see that she was safe and sound. Even Mrs McKitty gave her a cuddle.

Maisie thanked Sergeant MacStooshie for rescuing her. He introduced her to Doctor Purrkins.

"How do you do?" said Maisie. "Your Museum is a great place. It is full of surprises! I'm sorry I got locked in and caused a lot of bother, and I hope you don't mind me trying out the bicycle. I was VERY careful."

Doctor Purrkins smiled.

"That's good to hear, Maisie. Would you and Archie like to come back next Saturday morning? We have lots of special games and surprises for kittens then, and afterwards I can show you round."

Maisie and Archie said they would love to come.

Granny thanked Doctor Purrkins. "It is very kind of you to invite Maisie," she said. "She always means well, but I never know what she will do next."

"I know what she will be doing next," said Mrs McKitty. She had a few words with Doctor Purrkins, and went off to a cupboard under the stairs. When she came back, she was carrying a bucket and mop . . . and while the others went off to have tea and cake in the tea room, Maisie mopped and tidied, under Mrs McKitty's watchful eye, till the Museum was TICKETYBOO!

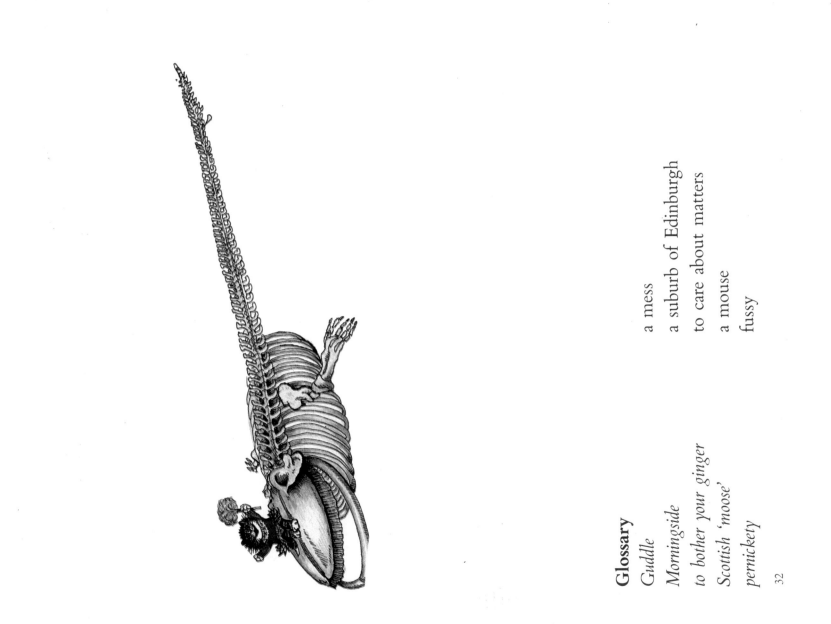

Glossary

Guddle   a mess

Morningside   a suburb of Edinburgh

to bother your ginger   to care about matters

Scottish 'moose'   a mouse

pernickety   fussy

"Excuse Me"

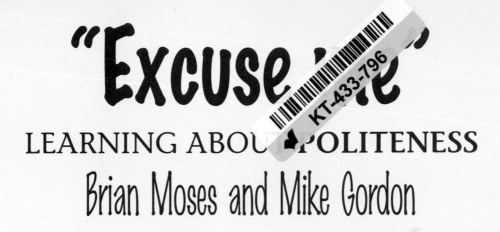

LEARNING ABOUT POLITENESS

Brian Moses and Mike Gordon

HODDER
Wayland

an imprint of Hodder Children's Books

The VALUES series:

"EXCUSE ME" LEARNING ABOUT **POLITENESS**
"I DON'T CARE!" LEARNING ABOUT **RESPECT**
"I'LL DO IT!" TAKING **RESPONSIBILITY**
"IT WASN'T ME!" LEARNING ABOUT **HONESTY**

Editor: Sarah Doughty
Designer: Malcolm Walker

First published in Great Britain in 1997 by
Wayland (Publishers) Ltd
Reprinted in 2001, 2002 and 2004 by Hodder Wayland,
an imprint of Hodder Children's Books
© Hodder Wayland 1997

Hodder Children's Books, a division of Hodder Headline Limited
338 Euston Road, London NW1 3BH

British Library Cataloguing in Publication Data
Moses, Brian, 1950 –
"Excuse me" : learning abiut politeness. – (Values)
1. Courtesy – Juvenile literature 2. Etiquette – Juvenile literature
I. Title II. Gordon, Mike, 1948 –
177.1

ISBN 0 7502 2138 0

Printed in China by WKT Company Ltd

CONTENTS

How polite are you?
When was the last time
you forgot your manners?

Was it lunchtime?

Was it yesterday when you didn't
give up your seat on the bus?

4

Was it last week when you were rude to mum's friend?

Or was it last year when you were much smaller and couldn't possibly be expected to behave properly ...

Let's just see how polite you really are.
Do you always remember to say 'please' and 'thank you' or do you sometimes behave like this ...

If you always try to say 'please' and 'thank you' then other people will know that you are grateful for what they do.

Thank you Mrs. Ford, that was a lovely tea.

You should always have good
manners at the meal table.

Ask someone to pass you
what you need, don't
make a grab for it.

Eat your food quietly, don't slurp
your soup.

Parents are fond of saying, 'Stop showing off'.

Sometimes this can happen at the meal table when visitors call for tea.

Sometimes it happens
when adults are talking.

Your parents will want to know that you have been behaving politely at school. Do not shout:

Can I go to the toilet; I'm desperate!

If you want to speak to your teacher remember to say 'please' and 'thank you' and ask quietly.

When you visit your friend's house to play, what do you take with you?

Your coat

Your bag

Your favourite toy ...

15

And if you're staying the night at your friend's house, you should be on your best behaviour.

I'll wait, Mr. Johnson, Toby can have his bath first.

17

Good manners are important if you are invited to someone's party ...

Not everyone can win a prize ... so don't throw a tantrum if you don't win the first game you play.

Just be patient and your turn
may come later.

When the party is over it is important to behave properly ...

Don't grab the party bag and rush out.

Make sure that you thank
your hosts for inviting you
to the party and tell them
that you enjoyed yourself.

Sometimes you might be invited to do something and be unable to go.

If this happens, you should refuse the invitation politely ...

Can you come on holiday with me this year? We're going to the seaside!

Don't hurt someone's feelings by saying that you'll be having a much more exciting time at Disneyland.

I'm very sorry but I'll be on holiday already that week.

If you have enjoyed yourself doing something with your friend's family, it is polite to write them a thank you note

Tell them how much you enjoyed yourself and how pleased you were to be invited.

You might even feel that you'd like to buy them a thank-you gift.

You should always be polite too when you are given a present yourself, even if it is something you already have ...

And even if it's something you don't really want ...

Be grateful for it.

Thank you, I'm sure it will be useful.

There's a lot to remember when it comes to being polite. How well do you do?

If you are polite, people remember you for all the right reasons.

So wherever you go, whatever you do ...
don't forget your manners.

NOTES FOR PARENTS AND TEACHERS

Prior to reading this book, ask children for examples of what they consider to be good and bad manners. Then read the book with children either individually or in groups and ask them the questions on page 4, 'When did you last forget your manners?' Talk about the answers that you receive. Develop these further by asking children to remember how people reacted to their bad manners. How did children feel about their bad behaviour after the event?

Children might like to act out some of the scenes in the book showing what happens when manners are forgotten. The scene could then be worked on again and changed so that we see how it develops when good manners are put into practice.

Compose rhymes or slogans with the children that remind them that manners are important. These could be read aloud along with hand claps or percussion instruments. For example:

Remember your 'pleases' (*four claps*)
Remember your 'thank yous' (*four claps*)
Remember your 'sorrys' (*four claps*)
These words make good children (*clap on each syllable*)

Talk about appropriate behaviour when at parties, visiting friends' houses, staying the night and so on. Ask children for their own anecdotes. Can they compose a list of rules regarding good manners that would apply to these situations?

Some children might like to write party invitations while others could compose polite letters of refusal. Others could act out phone conversations where they have to politely refuse an invitation to take part in a trip.

Ask children to illustrate the reminder 'Don't forget your manners'. Perhaps it will be a suitcase that's full of polite words, or maybe they'll think of another idea.

Explore manners further through the sharing of picture books mentioned in the book list.

BOOKS TO READ

'I Want My Dinner' by Tony Ross (Collins Picture Lions)
The Little Princess learns some manners but once she has mastered
'please' and 'thank you' she discovers that not everyone else is so
well-mannered.

'Max and the Magic Word' by Colin and Jacqui Hawkins (Viking Children's Books)
Max knows what he wants but not how to get it so his friends have to
teach him polite behaviour.

'The Elephant and the Bad Baby' by Elfrida Vipont, illustrated by
Raymond Briggs (Picture Puffin)
A tale about a baby who never says please.

'The Bad-Tempered Ladybird' by Eric Carle (Picture Puffin)
The bad-tempered ladybird is mean, rude and always trying to start a
fight but finally learns that it really pays to be polite.

'When Mum Turned into a Monster' by Joanna Harrison (Collins Picture
Lions)
A look at what can happen when children don't behave around the
home. Their rowdy behaviour makes mum so furious that she turns
into a monster!

INDEX